THE MAN INSIDE

THE MAN INSIDE

An Anthology of
writing and conversational
comment by men in prison

Edited by Tony Parker
Illustrations by Ken Ward

LONDON
MICHAEL JOSEPH

First published in Great Britain by Michael Joseph Ltd
52 Bedford Square, London, WC1
1973

ISBN 0 7181 0731 4

Photoset in Great Britain
by Filmtype Services Limited, Scarborough
in Century Medium ten on twelve point, and
printed by the Hollen Street Press, Slough

PREFACE

Cutting to avoid diffuseness and to preserve the flow of
the principal theme of a book is a necessary discipline;
and in television or radio programmes, in which the
length is decided in advance within limits to be counted
literally in seconds, it is a rigorous and at times brutally-
inescapable constriction. But after books based on tape-
recorded conversations are finished and when interviews
for television and radio are done, there is inevitably a
mass of residual material that has not been used; and
usually in the proportion that for every sentence printed
or broadcast there are at least fifty others which are
neither seen nor heard, for no other reason than that
space or time could not be found for them.

Also, if you go into prisons frequently over a period of
many years, talking with and listening to men confined
there, you will often be given things – pieces of writing
by men who find it easier to express themselves on paper
than in conversation, copies of poems, and written com-
munications of different kinds that are passed to you for
reasons having more to do with the security of an individual's privacy than any official regulations, many men
being so deeply immersed in prison sub-culture that they
go to great lengths to ensure none of their peers would
suspect them of ever having anything whatsoever to do
with outsiders. If you are additionally fortunate, some
prisoners may sometime feel confident enough to show
you are a treasured private possession, such as a notebook
or small sheaf of paper which they usually keep hidden
. . . "Little bits of me that nobody knows about". And if
you are even more fortunate still, you may be allowed to
copy out something from it.

It is from all these sources – fragments of conversations,
answers to questions, written notes and copies of private
writings – that this anthology has been constructed, in
the hope that it might convey not only something of what
being imprisoned means to prisoners but give some

indication as well of the variegated personalities of those concealed behind the blanket-categories of 'criminal', 'offender' or 'prisoner'. The criterion for inclusion has not of course been 'literary merit'; my concern has been with the words' content, the indication of thought and feeling revealed, sometimes only partially, by them – not primarily the facility with which they have been used. An ill-formed incoherence can often be more expressive than a carefully thought-out statement which has no spontaneity: the mastery of a technique sometimes blurs the genuine feeling it attempts to convey.

Although nearly all prisons at first sight appear uniformly drab and anonymous, and although many prisoners confined in them feel with good reason that being there erodes and diminishes their identity, not far beneath the surface a complex of multi-faceted personalities still exists. The range – both of thought and emotion, from the obsessive to the detached and from the savage to the gentle, and not only between one individual and another but within one and the same person – is extraordinary.

That prisoners spend much of their time thinking about themselves during the monotony and tedium of prison-life is not surprising; nor that they should think about prison itself and what is wrong with it and how it could be given more point or at least made less pointless – people who live outside think constantly about their occupation and situation, too. What is surprising is the number of times you can be surprised at discovering that 'criminals', 'offenders' and 'prisoners' are non-existent in any sense of total personalities. Harriet Martineau wrote as long ago as 1838 "The first principle seems to me to see the guilty as men – which they were before they were guilty, which they are in the midst of it, and which they will be when they are no longer so. Their humanity is the principal thing about them – their guilt is a temporary state." The fact that repeated proof of her insight can and still does surprise shows that the ability to accept it is defective, and as far as I am concerned the only small consola-

6

tion is the knowledge that others are perhaps similarly hampered. It may be I have spent too much time listening to prisoners, and not enough in trying to hear what they say. I hope others are more perceptive.

Men in prison say revealing things about themselves, about others, and about the effects of and faults in the penal system. Most importantly, they try to describe the effects it does not have – which are the ones most frequently stated as being intended and hoped-for by those who put them there; and it is not only the convicted prisoners who speak of this but prison staff. As those who put them there are us, and since we spend so much time, effort and money on doing it, we should perhaps listen – and make the attempt to try to hear what they say.

It was Robert Allerton, with whom I wrote *The Courage of His Convictions*, speaking from extensive personal experience who commented that the 'Omnibus' programme "Art In Prison" on which I worked for BBC Television with the director Geoff Baines, "gave more of the feel of what being in prison is like" than most things he had come across. Soon afterwards Leslie Cramphorn of Michael Joseph suggested that that programme's content might be used as a starting-point for an attempt to convey aspects of prison experience expressed by prisoners themselves, and his idea was encouraged by Richard Douglas-Boyd and Raleigh Trevelyan. My thanks are due to them; and profoundly to the men who said or wrote what is in this book. I am indebted most of all to my friend the late Douglas Gibson, and continually realise it. It was he who said to me "Shut up and listen to what prisoners say: when it comes to trying to understand, you won't – but do the best you can."

Tony Parker

For
ELIANE
in memory of Douglas
with love

THE MAN INSIDE

Royalties from the sale of this book will be
given to the Circle Trust

Do you know why you are doing it? You would say
You are doing it sadly out of regrettable necessity
And because you are unable to think of any alternative.
Perhaps in a moment of honesty you would admit too
That you are doing it in retaliation for the harm
And the anger we have caused you and your society.

Do you know what it is you are doing though?
Do you want to know or would you sooner not?
If you don't want to know though this still
Won't alter what are you are doing knowing or
    unknowing.

If you like to put it so we have demeaned others and
Therefore you are demeaning us. But you cannot
Separate us humans we are all indivisible and
Some of what you do to us you do to yourself.
You are not cleansing us, purging us, reforming us.
The anger and punishment you pour on us only
Generates retaliatory anger in us towards you
And the desire to get our own back. After all
We are not noble characters as you would be first to agree.
We do not ask for pity, sympathy, even forgiveness,
All we ask is that you think about what you are doing
And if you are satisfied go on but if you are not
Then stop. We cannot get out from the horizon-concealing
Walls you have confined us in. But you are freer
To consider in your situation such things as whether
Perhaps you too are also in a prison but a mental one.
Yes you put our bodies here for a sentence but our
Minds can and still do occasionally escape and fly free.
Do yours? Or are you serving a life-sentence in the
Terrible state of not even knowing you're doing it?

> Alan K. (29)
> Offence: using a firearm.
> Sentence: 10 years.

THE Streatfeild Committee emphasised the desirability and importance of sentencers visiting penal institutions. The best way of gaining knowledge of the conditions and training in such institutions is by visits, and by talks with governors, chaplains, medical officers, welfare officers and other members of the staff.

The Sentence of the Court: A Handbook for Courts on the Treatment of Offenders. H.M.S.O., 1971.

I'VE been in this prison eight years and no Judge has ever come here to my knowledge, and I'd say that's definite. There's no secrets in prison, if word hadn't been passed round beforehand we'd have heard it afterwards from one of the officers or someone. You could ask anyone here you like but no one would have heard of a Judge coming to this place.

Len B. (45)
Offence: manslaughter.
Sentence: 15 years.

A JUDGE? No mate, not in any prison I've been in and I've been in most of them in my time. No, wait a minute, now I come to think of it, yes there was talk of one having been to one place somewhere, but I think they all thought it was only a rumour. None of them had seen him, he hadn't talked to any of the prisoners or anything like that. If he did go I suppose he'd have been taken on a conducted tour for an hour and then gone away thinking he knew what it was like.

Joe R. (55)
Offence: housebreaking.
Sentence: 5 years.

GOING in a prison'll show you what one looks like, that's all. It won't give you any feeling what doing a sentence is like, and no one who's not served a sentence would have the faintest idea, they'd have no conception of it at all, how could they have?

Andy K. (36)
Offence: armed robbery.
Sentence: 8 years.

NOTHING could give it you unless you had the actual experience. Reading all the books there've ever been about prisons won't bring you anywhere near it, because they're mostly written by people who haven't been inside. Even those who have would only be writing about how it was to them anyway. I mean if you write a book or paint a picture or compose a piece of music what you're doing is recreating a personal experience and it'd be different to someone else. I've never read anything that made me feel whoever'd written it had got near to what it's like to me.
I suppose all I could say would be that when I die I might – I just might, though I doubt it – know what it's like to be dead. But I couldn't have any idea beforehand what it might be like because no one's written a book on being dead from personal experience. Those people that have written on prison from personal experience are different from most prisoners anyway because at least they can write even if it's badly, I mean put down on paper what they feel. But the majority of prisoners couldn't do that, so how does anyone know what they're feeling or suffering, or not feeling and not suffering.
All you know is they can't put it down on paper, but it wouldn't be safe to take it for granted therefore that nothing was going on inside them.

Roy S. (48)
Offence: murder.
Sentence: life.

I REMEMBER one time when I was out a good few years back, between some of my early sentences, and I was living with a girl and she was always asking me "What's prison like?" At first I just used to say "It's fucking horrible" or "It's fucking terrible" but she wouldn't let it rest, she used to keep on and on, she'd say "Yes, but what's it really *like*?" Eventually one day I said "Look, anyone who keeps asking what it's like couldn't understand it even if it could be explained to them", so she shut up then. A few months later I was nicked and back in prison again and I sent her a letter, one of the blank sheets of lined paper they give you with only your name and number and the address of the prison printed on it. I wrote right across it "This is what it's like. I hope you understand now." I don't think she did, because she never replied.

Jack Y. (42)
Offence: receiving.
Sentence: 5 years.

I READ something in a book sometime, about it was like you were a man trying to crawl to safety up the tilting deck of a ship as it was slowly sinking on its side into the water, and I think that's the nearest I can say to it. Only there was more to it, that he didn't put – that the ship never finally sinks and it never comes upright again either, so you don't drown but you don't survive. It's more like you're perpetually in between the two, living a completely sideways life, and you know it's sideways but you can't do anything to make any difference to it.

Bob D. (35)
Offence: robbery with violence.
Sentence: 10 years.

I DON'T think you could say
being in prison is like anything,
because being in prison you're a
big nothing in the middle of a big
nothing, and that's not 'like'
anything.

> Malcolm J. (28)
> Offence: fraud.
> Sentence: 4 years.

THE real prison isn't a drab Victorian building, overcrowded and noisy and smelly and depressing. And it isn't a modernly-built place like some that exist now with a bit of coloured paintwork and a few flower-beds and with bars that are patterned. Neither of these is the real prison.

The real prison is lack of freedom, loneliness, sickness of soul, an atmosphere that is a breeding-ground for bitterness and a hatchery for hate. This is the real prison.

Stuart H. (24)
Offence: arson.
Sentence: 4 years.

PEOPLE talk about prison being a deterrent, they say things like "I wouldn't do such-and-such because I'd be frightened of getting caught and sent to prison for it". But the fact of the matter is hardly anyone gets sent to prison for a first offence unless it's something very serious: if they've got no previous record they're fined or put on probation or something. Most of the people who actually go to prison have usually got a fair amount of institutional experience behind them – they might have been in children's homes when they were young, approved schools, borstals, detention centres and the rest – and for them prison's one more step along the line, simply another variation of being in custody. The thought of being in it once more can hardly be much of a deterrent in their case. Most of them spend far more time thinking of ways to do things without being caught than they ever do of the consequences.

So it's ridiculous to think it's a deterrent, it's merely an admission of defeat by society, because I shouldn't think there's one person in a thousand who goes straight to prison for a first offence – and that's a very low proportion indeed to have to have such an expensive deterrent for.

Walter C. (54)
Offence: embezzlement.
Sentence: 6 years.

I'D no previous record, I'd never been in any kind of trouble, and between committing the offence and my trial I was out on bail. One day I was just walking around like any ordinary person, and the next I was in prison starting a four-year sentence.

My case was the last one heard in the afternoon and the prison I went to was a long way from the court so I didn't reach it until late at night. It was an unbelievable experience, absolutely terrifying. For some reason I was taken through the main prison first before reaching the reception-part where I was to be booked-in and given my uniform and all the rest of it. They took me in along a huge gloomy hall, very narrow and high, with hardly any lights in it, but I could see it reached up for about four or five floors with hundreds of cell doors all shut on every landing. There were a few prison officers standing about on the different levels but no one else to be seen at all. It took a long time for it to dawn on me there was a man locked-up behind every one of the doors. Eventually we came to a circular part called "The Centre" and when we got there I saw there were another four halls all exactly the same as the one I'd come along, radiating off from it. I can remember thinking 'Jesus Christ, there must be hundreds and hundreds of men locked-up in all those cells, how can there be anything individual or personal in a place like this?' Then I thought 'Oh my God, and I'm going to be one of them. I haven't been here five minutes and I've already completely lost any identity.' And I started to shiver, I lost all control and I did, I wet myself.

Stuart H. (24)
Offence: arson.
Sentence: 4 years.

NO matter how many times I've
been in prison the most
horrible and degrading part of it is
always the reception procedure.
You're entered on a form, all the
things you've got that are going to
be taken off you are listed on
another form, and then you have to
sign. It makes you feel like you're
signing your whole personality
away. And you are too.

Steve P. (35)
Offence: possessing firearms.
Sentence: 5 years.

IT'S as though it'd all been very carefully thought out as a deliberate way to humiliate you. First they write down all the details of you, then they take your personal possessions and seal them up in a packet, then they take your clothes off you and put them in a numbered box, and finally you end-up standing there with just a towel round your waist. What they're doing is reducing your identity stage by stage, slowly wiping you out as a person until you're only one more piece of flesh with a name and number. It's frightening to have it done to you, to realise how easily it can be done, how completely powerless you are to prevent them taking away your individuality.

Ron G. (26)
Offence: possession of drugs.
Sentence: 4 years.

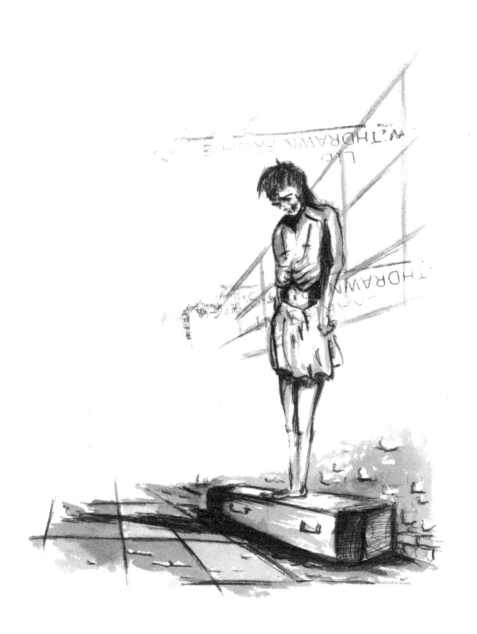

DEPERSONALISATION – that's the whole principle behind it. Everything's taken from you and put away in store until the time for your release, and you don't get it back till then. Everything, including your personality, except that's the one thing which isn't handed back again because it doesn't exist anymore.

Philip B. (38)
Offence: malicious wounding.
Sentence: 6 years.

Height
Weight
Colour of eyes
Colour of hair
Date of birth –
They map it all,
My physical earth.

"Sign for it here
And sign for it there."

Mind
Dreams
Aspects of hope
Darkness of fear
Heart of a man –
They do not draw
Any human diagram.

"Sign for it there
And sign for it here."

Peeling off the exterior
Before admission to the interior
To ensure the feeling
Of being thoroughly inferior.

> Terry J. (25)
> Offence: dangerous driving.
> Sentence: 4 years.

YOU get shunted around a lot from one prison to another if you're doing a long sentence. It can be for any number of reasons – what they consider to be for your good, or their good, or something to do with overcrowding or reclassifying you, or for no good reason whatever as far as you can tell. Up to now I've been in eleven different prisons in six years. There are slight differences in the scenery sometimes, but one thing never changes and that's the reception bit you have to go through whenever you get to another prison. I can't help thinking sometimes that moving you's done deliberately for no other reason than to put you through that whole disgusting business so you'll keep getting regular reminders that in their eyes you're no more than a parcel of shit.

Roger L. (31)
Offence: armed robbery.
Sentence: 12 years.

YOU know, right from the start of it when we first come in I think we each likes to be treat as though he was human, just a bit. Because we is, all of us is, no matter what we done, I mean thieves or frauders or taking away motor-cars, rapers even murderers is all human. Punished, yes, I think we all agrees what we done is to be punished for. Only there is still a bit human in us even if only a little bit, but straight off we all get throwed in one big heap the first day we arrive and I think it get squashed right down out of sight specially if what we've got in us that's human is only that very little bit.

Eddie S. (47)
Offence: indecent assault.
Sentence: 8 years.

"We're sending you to a new prison"
The Governor said. (He didn't mean it,
It was 'different' he meant.)
So I came to this new prison and it wasn't even
Any different. Arrived, stripped, searched,
Told to have a bath, given another uniform.
First night in my cell a screw came and said
"Settling-in, son?" Jesus fucking hell . . .

This isn't me you've got here you know.
You might call me a new prisoner or a different one
But I'm neither. As far as you're concerned
I'm merely another body for you to file-away
In a spare cell while I sit here swearing and
Saying (correctly this time): Oh no, non-fucking hell.

Well I'll repeat it though you couldn't care –
This isn't me you've got here. I was lost somewhere
Back there at some time or another
While you were ticking me off, signing for me
And all that. Don't ask me where I've gone,
I hadn't even noticed my disappearance myself.

I suppose I must still be lying around somewhere
On some dusty and completely forgotten shelf.
But don't bother to go looking, because
I couldn't tell you where to begin.
I only know that I'm "settling-in" well
In this not-new and not-different cell.
So what the fucking or the non-fucking hell?

Les M. (34)
Offence: housebreaking.
Sentence: 6 years.

PRISON work's simply a way of passing time. I don't know why the authorities aren't brave enough to come right out with it and say that's what it is and all it's meant to be, instead of trying to deceive the public into believing it has a value and that something's happening when it isn't. If you take the majority of the prison population basically it's made up of only two kinds of prisoner – those who've got no skills whatsoever and are virtually unemployable, and those who could work if they wanted to but prefer to live by crime. They've no intention of going straight when they get out, and all they think about while they're in is how to get away with it next time. Talk about teaching a 'work-pattern' to anyone is rubbish – the first category could never learn one, and the second don't want to. To be realistic we ought to leave both sorts to their own devices, let them read books or watch television or play games all day, and concentrate all our very limited resources on providing decent work for those who are capable of doing it and interested in it.

Principal Prison Officer (51)
20 years' service.

WORK in prison has two main purposes. One is to try and keep the prisoners occupied, and the other much more important one is to keep the prison functioning. Well over fifty percent of it – cleaning, laundry, gardening, painting, building, repairing, making clothes and shoes and bedding, cooking – it's all connected with running the prison, and if it wasn't done by the prisoners the whole place would grind to a halt.

It can be summed-up very simply by saying there'll always have to be a steady supply of prisoners to provide the labour-force to enable prisons to cope with the steady supply of prisoners.

Walter C. (54)
Offence: embezzlement.
Sentence: 6 years.

SPEAKING from the experience of all the times I've been in, it's not likely you'd get through any sentence without being put to sewing mail-bags at some time, often because they can't find anything else for you to do. Usually you do it by hand, eight stitches to the inch – no more and no less – with a rough thread which you first of all have to pull across a lump of black wax before you use it. Then when you finish one bag you put it on a pile of others and start on a fresh one. They have sewing-machines in the workshops but they're not keen on you using them because that does the job too quickly and then there aren't enough bags to go round. I've known it happen many times that if they're very short of bags waiting to be sewn you'll be made to unpick one you've just finished and start it all over again.

Mike O. (40)
Offence: warehouse breaking.
Sentence: 4 years.

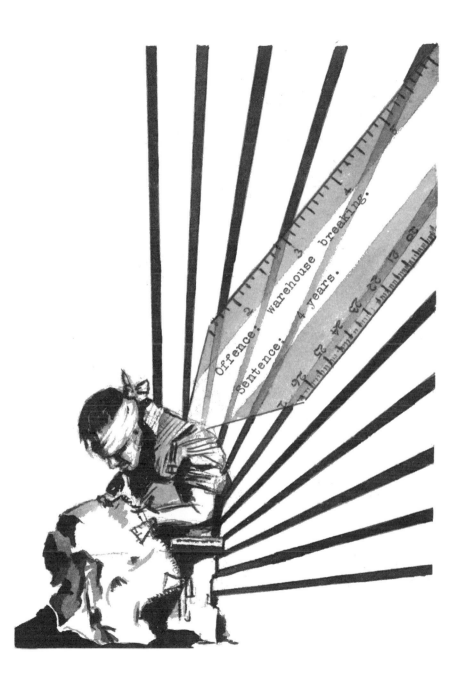

Here I am, sewing . . .
A stitch in time?
No, it isn't going to stop me
Having to sew the other
Nine million ninety-nine thousand
Nine hundred and ninety-nine.

Peter D. (28)
Offence: larceny.
Sentence: 3 years.

IT doesn't matter whether you're brainy and intelligent or completely thick and stupid. There aren't any jobs in prison which you need to be brainy and intelligent for, so you become thick and stupid even if you weren't like that to start with.

> Graham G. (29)
> Offence: fraud.
> Sentence: 4 years.

THERE'S a lot of us in prison who've never had no chance to learn to work, because I think the only way a man can learn how to work is if you give him work that's interesting and he's interested in doing and likes doing it because it's interesting. I don't see how scrubbing floors and sewing mail-bags and things like that is ever going to make anybody like work because it's not interesting, in fact I think it's going to do just the opposite and make him not like work if he thinks that's all work is, something he's got to do but isn't interesting, it won't make him think work is a good thing will it?

John N. (35)
Offence: housebreaking.
Sentence: 5 years.

NO one learns anything that will be any help to them when they go out. I'm not aware, for instance, that there's an insatiable demand at good rates of pay for men who can scrub and clean and polish, or make roughly-fitting shoes or brushes, or boil hundredweights of cabbage and potatoes. Really it's beyond me why they don't do things like buying-up old motor-cars and teaching men the rudiments of being garage mechanics, show them how to rewire a house, repair television sets, or make tables and chairs – anything that's got at least some connection with some sort of job they might get outside. Or it could be clerical work, book-keeping, filing, indexing, store-keeping. The ridiculous thing is it'd hardly cost them anything: there are plenty of men serving sentences themselves who could be put to teaching things like that, which they already know about, to others. So as well as passing on their knowledge they'd be usefully employed themselves while they were in, instead of being kept pointlessly occupied at the tax-payers' expense.

Walter C. (54)
Offence: embezzlement.
Sentence: 6 years.

THE latest stupid idea someone's thought up now is something they're calling an "industrial prison", built along the lines of a factory with modern plant and equipment for paint-spraying and sheet-metal work and God knows what else. Men who go there work a forty-five hour week or something like that, with overtime and piece-rates and bonuses. It's said to be like a proper outside factory, no different at all, and the idea's to give a man the feel of working for his living as a realistic preparation for getting a job on release. Only selected prisoners go there, who are thought to be most likely to benefit from the experience and work for their living when they go out.

But what's not mentioned unless it has to be is that men there still aren't paid proper wages, only a pound a week or a bit more, they don't have stamped insurance cards, so they get no true idea of the cost of living or how to handle money. No thought's given to a man's underlying problems that made him criminal or to the fact that however well he works there it's in a sheltered atmosphere that's not at all like outside really. And the other big snag about it is that those who get selected for it are usually the ones best able to con the authorities into putting them into a slightly better prison by pretending they intend to go straight in the future.

Bob D. (35)
Offence: robbery with violence.
Sentence: 10 years.

I WONDER why they don't set-up cigarette-factories in prisons to produce a supply of cheap cigarettes for smoking by prisoners? It'd provide work for those making them, and do away with the biggest single cause of trouble in all prisons which is the shortage of tobacco. Tobacco's the currency of the penal system because nobody can afford enough on what they earn, so if you deflated its value it'd save a tremendous amount of aggravation, it would.

Ken L. (24)
Offence: assault on police.
Sentence: 4 years.

THE work isn't taxing enough, I mean mentally not physically. It's boring, it doesn't bring any satisfaction, it doesn't make you use your brain, so your mind wanders off into unreality because you've got no problems about food or clothes or somewhere to live or anything. And there's nothing you can do will make any difference to when you're going to be let out, you fall back into inertia and concentrate on not misbehaving so that you'll be given your full remission. I think that's all very negative, I don't think you should get remission just because you've done nothing. You ought to have to earn it by your own efforts, either mental or physical, and at least that'd stimulate you into activity if you felt there were opportunities for doing things that had some bearing on when you'd be released. And I'm not talking about myself, I'm talking about the fixed-sentence men: the day they come in they know the earliest date they can get out, which I think is bad because it doesn't encourage them to stir themselves in any way.

Pat D. (42)
Offence: murder.
Sentence: life.

SOME people say prisons are non-productive. They aren't. There's one thing they produce thousands and thousands of to perfection – cabbages.

> Tom G. (46)
> Offence: fraud.
> Sentence: 7 years.

EVERY single thing that happens
is ordained for you from above
– when you get up, when you go to
bed, when you start work, when you
stop, when you eat, have a bath,
write a letter, see a visitor,
everything. All that matters is you
do what you're told when you're
told. I was put inside for being
irresponsible in the eyes of society –
and put into the most
irresponsible way of life I've ever
led.

Ron G. (26)
Offence: possession of drugs.
Sentence: 4 years.

I DON'T see how it can avoid the effect of making you hate authority. Authority's all round you, every minute of the day and night, you can't do anything at all unless it says so, wherever you turn it's standing there looking at you. And its fundamental purpose is not to help you but to keep you away from society. So what else could anyone possibly feel about it but hate?

> Victor G. (40)
> Offence: armed robbery.
> Sentence: 10 years.

I'VE never met any kind of man who frightens me so much as a prison officer. I can't even begin to imagine how human beings can do to other human beings what they do, lock them up at certain times and unlock them at others, order them around all day, keep on counting them, and carry on all the time as though they were dealing with a lot of animals. Most of them aren't cruel, it isn't that, they're just totally impersonal and feelingless day after day and for years on end. I suppose when they're off duty they have wives and families so presumably they must have some human qualities, but if they have then I can't understand how they stick their job.

> Derek P. (38)
> Offence: receiving.
> Sentence: 4 years.

THERE'VE been times, many of them, when I've hated the screws so much it's been just like having a pain. One'll tell you to do something and you get this feeling rising up inside you, in your stomach and your chest and head, and you think what you'd like to do to him. And what you'd like to do is plain and simple and straightforward – you'd like to kill him stone dead. At that moment if you had a gun or a knife you would kill him. But you haven't so you go away and think out plans for killing him, hour after hour you think about it because your mind's so poisoned with hate . . . all because he told you to do something like go and get a bucket.

Roy S. (48)
Offence: murder.
Sentence: life.

YOU'LL hear plenty of prisoners say there's no such thing as a 'good' screw, a lot of the less-original minded of them never fail to put the letters 'A.S.A.B.' on the back of the envelope of every letter they send out. It stands for 'All Screws Are Bastards'. I'd be inclined to agree with them. I don't think most of us are anything else but bastards, otherwise we wouldn't be screws. But then there aren't all that many prisoners who are what you might call exactly shining examples of unblemished purity.

Prison Officer (36)
8 years' service.

LATELY I've started wondering
where all the decent or the at
least not-too-bad screws have got
to. I'm sure there used to be some
nicer ones around when I first
come into this place. Maybe it's like
what people say about policemen,
when you start thinking how young
they're getting all it means is that
it's you that's getting old. But it's
not quite the same though, it's not
I notice younger screws, there
don't seem to be any other kind but
real nasty ones now.

Len B. (45)
Offence: manslaughter.
Sentence: 15 years.

THERE are one or two screws that I might go so far as to have a drink with if I met them in a pub when I was out. But it is only one or two, all the rest I've nothing but contempt for, absolute loathing for. If I ever got the chance I'd think no more of squashing the life out of them than I would of treading on a beetle.

> Steve P. (35)
> Offence: possessing firearms.
> Sentence: 5 years.

IF you work up to your neck in shit all day you're bound to stink a bit yourself aren't you?

> Prison Officer. (32)
> 3 years' service.

ASK a screw why he became a screw, unless he thinks you're a mad halfwit he wouldn't tell you it was because he wanted to try and help people, he knows if he did all you'd do is laugh. Probably he'll say something neutral like it was for the security, a job with a house and a pension at the end of it. That won't be the truth of course, because there's other things he could have done if that was all he was after. It might be hard to believe but there's no other alternative, it must be because they like it. And if they do then they can't be anything else at heart but sadists.

> Harry M. (42)
> Offence: fraud.
> Sentence: 12 years.

I CAME into the service because I was brought-up in an orphanage, I went straight from there into the army, and I was captured soon after the war started and spent nearly six years in a prisoner-of-war camp. When I came home again I knew I couldn't live any life except in some kind of institution so I didn't even hesitate about applying. It's never crossed my mind to think about anything else and it never will.

Prison Officer (48)
15 years' service.

I THINK some officers did perhaps come into it thinking they might do some good and genuinely believing it was a way of helping people. But after a few years they either can't stand it and leave, or they let themselves lapse into being thoughtless automatons because that's the only way they can carry on. When they get older and start reaching near the end of their time they might be a bit fatherly and slap-dash and not bothering, but that's because by then they can afford to relax and let their juniors do most of the dirty work.

Trevor T. (49)
Offence: fraud.
Sentence: 8 years.

I WORK all my life inside these walls and when I go home it's to a house just outside them where I see the same walls but from the other side, that's all. I often find myself thinking 'Well at least every prisoner knows the date when he won't have to look at them any more, which is more than I do.'

Prison Officer (40)
9 years' service.

BOTH the prisoners and the general public look down on us, but somebody's got to do the job though we don't get any respect or thanks for it from anyone. Every day of our working life we have to mix with very difficult and sometimes dangerous people – but we weren't responsible for putting them in prison, we've got no say in when they go out, all we've got to do is keep them there. I think the prisoners despise us because we represent the public, and I think the public despises us because we're doing what they want us to in their hearts but they try to pretend they don't. It's like the same way they look down on lavatory attendants or dustmen: they couldn't do without them but they wouldn't soil their own hands doing their job.

Prison Officer (36)
9 years' service.

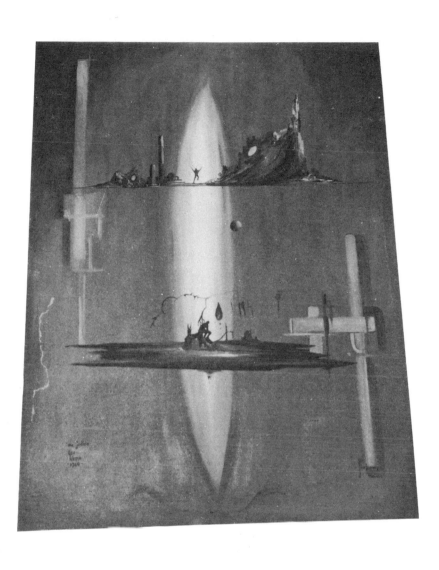

I REALLY do enjoy my work. I don't like the locking and the unlocking and the counting and all that bullshit, but our lords and masters say it's got to be done so I do it as best I can without thinking about it. The part I enjoy is mixing with criminals and I don't mind saying it. I don't mean it gives me a thrill because it's not very thrilling, most of them being ordinary characters more or less like I am. But I do like their company, I feel at ease with them, I'd sooner be with them any evening than sitting in a pub or watching television. They're not much worse than I am and I'm not much better than they are. I could easily have turned-out a criminal myself if I'd had a different background or circumstances, or whatever it is sends some people one way and others another.

Prison Officer (39)
11 years' service.

YOU get optimists, pessimists, introverts, extroverts, all sorts just like you would anywhere else. Philosophers, bitter twisted characters, those who complain all the time, those who never complain whatever happens. You can't be a person who works in a prison for long without realising what a terrible waste of time it all is, how men with brains and feelings and hearts are being ruined simply by the struggle to stay alive in the face of all the stupid restrictions and regulations they're surrounded with. If only half the energy they had to devote to battling in their minds against that sort of thing could be put to some constructive use I'd say you might even get something worthwhile out of prisons. But under the present system there's not a hope: the important things are ignored and the petty things are all-important.

Prison Welfare Officer (32)
Seconded from Probation
Service.

Raed Knalb, I thought
siht dluow ekam a
egnahc yawyna
    Sruoy ylerecnis,
    Nor

YOU'RE allowed to write one letter a week, but what the hell is there to write about? "We scrubbed the corridor yesterday, it looks terrific. We had a great time in the tailoring shop last Tuesday, we made our one-millionth pair of prison-uniform trousers. I was walking round the yard on exercise today and I completed seventeen circuits before it started to rain and we were brought inside." You couldn't say it was exactly compulsive reading for someone who got it, could you? If you were honest all you'd write would be "Dear Blank, I hope you are well. I'm dead. Yours sincerely." They could have a printed form to save you writing it, then everyone'd be saved a lot of time.

Ron G. (26)
Offence: possession of drugs.
Sentence: 4 years.

I NEVER know what to put in letters, sometimes I just send out nothing but a list of questions, not because I want to know the answers but because I can't think of anything to say. Once I wrote to my mother "What size of shoes do you take, how much did my sister Eileen weigh when she was born, and how long does it take to get from North Finchley to South Croydon by 'bus?" She rang up the prison saying she thought I was going off my head and I ought to be seen by a psychiatrist.

Graham G. (29)
Offence: fraud.
Sentence: 4 years.

LETTERS in and out are all censored and they can be stopped if they're considered 'objectionable'. That means you can write things like "The Governor is a very fine man" as often as you like, but you mustn't put something which might be true like "The Chaplain's a pompous fat pig." I used to write to a girl "I think of you every night before I go to sleep" and nobody bothered: then one day I wrote "I wish you were here so I could fuck you" and a screw came rushing in my cell to tell me I couldn't send it. They're not all that fussy the other way round, once when my wife wrote "You're the biggest lousy lying bastard I know" nobody stopped that on the grounds I might think it was objectionable.

Ron C. (39)
Offence: housebreaking.
Sentence: 5 years.

I SUPPOSE there must be censorship, but if there is I don't see why it can't be done by someone who never sees you and seals it up again after it's been read. There's an officer here calls you into his office to tell you there's a letter, then he makes you stand there while he reads it and keeps giving little sarcastic laughs at things in it. Another habit he's got is handing you a letter in its opened envelope so you can see he's carefully crossed out the "Mr." on it in front of your name.

Gordon P. (44)
Offence: receiving.
Sentence: 5 years.

MAYBE your wife tells you she's had enough, she's got someone else, she's leaving you. You write her to plead with her to give you another chance. The next day a screw'll say "That letter you wrote your wife, you'll be lucky!" Then a few days later he says "Here you are, what did I tell you?" and hands you her reply. In some sort of way he might even be meaning it well, but it's a bit much to expect anyone to appreciate it.

> Ted R. (35)
> Offence: warehouse breaking.
> Sentence: 3 years.

YOU'VE got to forget about it, that all your letters are read and you haven't any rights to secrets or personal feelings. If an officer makes any comment about anything you've written you've got to ignore it completely, otherwise you'd never be able to write anything to anyone.

Ian S. (40)
Offence: forgery.
Sentence: 5 years.

I DON'T get many letters but if I do get one I read it every day for weeks till I've learned it absolutely off by heart and then I repeat it to myself in bed at night. Then it might be a few months later and I get another one, so then I start to learn that one instead.

> Joe R. (55)
> Offence: housebreaking.
> Sentence: 5 years.

I wanted to send you roses –
   only they don't sell flowers here
   but they said I could have some free thorns.

I wanted to send you a bracelet –
   only they don't sell jewellery here
   but they said I could have some spare chains.

I wanted to send you a wrist-watch –
   only they don't sell time-pieces here
   but they said I could give you some empty hours.

I wanted to send you a dress –
   only they don't sell clothing here
   but they said I could give you a repaired mail-bag.

I wanted to give you a kiss –
   and they were very helpful about that.
   They said there was a fellow going out next week
   and he'd give it you if I gave him your name and
   address.

                    Paul M. (28)
                    Offence: grievous bodily harm.
                    Sentence: 6 years.

APART from the date of your release the only thing you live for in prison is your visits. You have a half-hour visit once a month, and you live from month to month because that's the only time you see someone who's connected with you and not with anyone else.

Barry F. (34)
Offence: larceny.
Sentence: 5 years.

YOU say "My husband's in prison" and people get this look on their faces, they sort of draw back as if it's some dreadful disease they think they're standing next to. I could shake them, I want to say "You should meet my husband, he's not a thoroughly bad sort of person, in fact he's a very kind and gentle sort of person." And when you tell them you can go and see him and you do go and see him as often as they'll let you, they look surprised, as though they can't understand how you could want to.

Wife of prisoner
serving 4 years.

EVERY time, he says "How are things?" and I always say "Oh everything's fine." I don't tell him about being behind with the rent or having to take one of the kids to the doctor or that someone's kicked a football through the kitchen window and I can't afford to have it mended. But he's not stupid, he says "Well you look worried, what's the matter?" so I say "Oh it's just I'm not sleeping very well" or something like that. Because I don't want him to worry about me, that won't help him get through it, which is my main concern. I keep asking him if he's all right and he always says he is but I know bloody well he's not. There'll be times when we both sit there the full half-hour like that, telling each other we're fine. We both know we're lying like hell but what else can we say?

Wife of prisoner
serving 7 years.

THE ones I envy are the unmarried ones. You feel terrible if you've got a wife and kids because you know how much it's hurting them, they're doing the sentence just as much as you are. You can't forget them and you know they can't forget you and it hurts all the time, it never stops.

> Les M. (34)
> Offence: housebreaking.
> Sentence: 6 years.

WHEN it's an open visit you come face to face with your wife across a table, there are other prisoners sitting all round and screws only a couple of feet away, so what can you really talk about? It doesn't feel like you're in contact at all, and you're not, you're strangers. Every time she comes now it gets worse, I feel we're drifting further and further apart, and we are.

Gordon P. (44)
Offence: receiving.
Sentence: 5 years.

I try to see you
But I can't.
I try to hold you
But I can't.
I try to keep you
But I can't.

I can only see me,
I can only hold on to me,
I can only keep myself
To myself, that's as much
As I can do.

Doing time I haven't mental time
For you, can only try to keep
Something of myself living
For giving back to you again
One day. But I wonder
If there's any point when
I don't know what
Will have happened to you
By then?

Derek P. (38)
Offence: receiving.
Sentence: 4 years.

You smiled
   and it was pleasant to
   see you smile, it wasn't a
      "You-made-the-sun-shine"
   sort of smile . . .
But I must say
the rest of the day
seemed somehow warm.

You spoke
   and it was pleasant to
   hear you speak, it wasn't the
      "Let's-talk-about-me"
   sort of talk . . .
But I must say
the rest of the day
was spent thinking about you.

You cried
   and it was sad to
   hear you cry, it wasn't a
      "I'm-lonely-nobody-cares"
   sort of cry . . .
But I could find no smile or words
with which to try and comfort you.

And I must say
the rest of the day
seemed somehow useless.

Ralph H. (33)
Offence: housebreaking.
Sentence: 4 years.

81

I CAN'T help it, I hate visits. I can't tell her not to come, I suppose she wants to, but I get choked. I mean I've got another eight years still to do, I don't want to hear about what's going on outside, what she said, what someone else said, how so-and-so is. It doesn't concern me, how can it possibly concern me? When she came today what she was talking about was the present, and that means nothing at all. She was saying things about what happened last week, what's going to happen next week: to her, and to people she knows. But nothing happened to me last week and nothing's going to happen next week, so what else could it be but a completely fucking ridiculous one-sided conversation? The most I wanted was just to look at her, remind myself what she looked like, not to talk or to listen. Now it's what, three hours later, I haven't the remotest idea of a single word she said.

Danny A. (35)
Offence: armed robbery.
Sentence: 14 years.

AFTER a visit someone's bound to say to you, perhaps another prisoner or a screw, "How did it go, did you have a good visit?" You always say "Oh yeah, great". But many a time I've only just managed to force myself to say it instead of doing what I really felt like which was smashing him in the face.

Victor G. (40)
Offence: armed robbery.
Sentence: 10 years.

C

INSIDE you spend all your time trying not to think about outside, but it's when you get a visit that you can't avoid it. Whoever it is who comes, they don't seem to be who they are, but more like people who remind you of someone you used to know when you were out.

Arthur B. (32)
Offence: possessing firearms.
Sentence: 5 years.

NO I've never had a visit from no-one for over ten years now, no not a letter or a Christmas card or a birthday card or anything. I don't know no-one you see, that's why.

Alf B. (50)
Offence: rape
Sentence: life.

SOME of them do try to keep their minds alive by reading books, and some of them are even more positive than that and create things, paint pictures or write poems. They might not be particularly good pictures or poems but at least they're trying to express something of themselves. Some of them manage occasionally to be quite humourous too, though how they manage that in these places God only knows.

Assistant Governor.
8 years' service.

As I was musing one day
Sad and lonely
Without a friend,
Suddenly from out of the blue
A voice came to me saying
'Cheer up!
Things could be worse!'

So I cheered up
And sure enough
Things did get worse.

Ralph H. (33)
Offence: housebreaking.
Sentence: 4 years.

I'm fed-up with this gaol:
I never get any mail.
My life is wasting away
Day after day.

I wonder if she'll wait
And be there to meet me at the gate?
It is, it's driving me insane:
Definitely, I'll never get in trouble again.

When you're doing a very long time
You are very sorry indeed for your crime.
And I for one shall certainly change my ways
When I've finished doing my seven days.

> Ken L. (24)
> Offence: assault on police.
> Sentence: 4 years.

My cell is nice, so's every screw.
My ceiling's white, the walls are blue.
It's sometimes said the staff are bad,
But that's not true, they're like my Dad.
Why, the Chief is such a pleasant chap
He plays with us upon his lap.
And the Governor's truly idolised
By cons like me – the institutionalised.

> Les M. (34)
> Offence: housebreaking
> Sentence: 6 years.

I WRITE things down on scraps of paper in the night in the dark. I've had a lot of practice at it. Words, phrases, fragments, ideas for poems perhaps. Little bits of me that nobody knows about and I keep hidden.

> Ian S. (40)
> Offence: forgery.
> Sentence: 5 years.

A work of art
is your hair
cascading down your back

A work of art
is a tank slowly burning
in a Prague doorway

A work of art
is a teddy-bear lying
beside a cot of love

A work of art
is a machine which
reproduces the sound of crying

A work of art
is a note played endlessly
on a piano just out of earshot

A work of art
is you
or haven't I told you?

          Paul M. (28)
          Offence: grievous bodily harm.
          Sentence: 6 years.

One of these days
we will be shy when we meet
and look away
knowing that we don't know what to say.

But we will find words to share
and enjoy them together
and you will tell me your things
and I will tell you mine.

And then before long
we will dare to hold hands
and walk together and be together
and miss each other when we part.

And there will come a time when we lie together
and I will caress you and your smooth skin
to show you that I love you.

Sometime, somewhere . . . whoever you are.

Alan K. (29)
Offence: using a firearm.
Sentence: 10 years.

MOST of them's better educated than me but I like reading but it's not easy. I'm trying to read a book now by somebody called Steinbeck, John Steinbeck I think he's called. I lay in bed each night and have a read of it and I keep a dictionary next me so I can look up words. Only what does me is I can't seem to remember them, I'll find out what something means and then a few pages later I come across that same word and I've forgotten again. I might have to look up the same word sometimes ten times in one evening. I'd like to read more but it's hard, it gets you down going on like that, sometimes I get bloody furious and give up and chuck the book across the cell.

Alf B. (50)
Offence: rape.
Sentence: life.

I'LL read any book that's called "The Complete Works". I don't mind who it's by but I like that title, as soon as I see any book called that in the library I borrow it. I can't think of any particular authors' names but if they've ever written anything with the title "The Complete Works" it's fairly certain I'll have read it.

Brian C. (34)
Offence: larceny.
Sentence: 5 years.

I'D never read a book in my life till I came in here. So having a big sentence I thought I might as well start, and I've read hundreds now. Books have introduced me to all sorts of things I never knew existed – ideas, the way different people think about different things, music, art, religion, history, politics. A whole new world's woken-up inside me. All my life before I'd just been existing, not thinking or seeing or being aware of anything. It's exactly like being born and coming alive. And I think oh Jesus what a place to have to come in to, to come alive.

Dick M. (32)
Offence: attempted murder.
Sentence: 15 years.

I GET these terrific bursts of wanting to paint. I do one picture, then another, then another, and I can't wait for the paint to dry on one or stop to look at it before I start the next. I'm right out of this world, I'm possessed, up in space somewhere, completely free for hours. Then suddenly the light goes out, I'm in pitch dark, I know I'm just a prisoner in a prison then.

Frank E. (30)
Offence: housebreaking.
Sentence: 6 years.

WHEN you've been inside a
long time you forget what
things like hills and fields look like.
Now and again I ask the art-class
teacher if he'll go up on the moors
and look at the scenery through my
eyes for me. When he comes back
and tells me about it, I try to paint
it.

John E. (34)
Offence: manslaughter.
Sentence: 10 years.

I DO paint, but I keep my pictures in my cell. Sometimes in the night I get up and strike matches and look at a few of them. I like doing that, seeing them in that sort of faint glow, it makes them look mellow and old like they were painted a long time ago by one of the Old Masters, and it makes them seem much better than they really are.

Arthur B. (32)
Offence: possessing firearms.
Sentence: 5 years.

I THINK you'll find more bitterness and self-pity in prisons than in any other place on earth, because prisons are the nearest things to hells-on-earth that have ever been created. To people who can't stand bitterness or think there's something distasteful about self-pity, all I'd say is "Well stop and ask yourself if you're sure you're such a fine character that you wouldn't be like that yourself if you were inside?" If their answer was they're sure they wouldn't, I'd think they'd very little imagination and no self-knowledge.

Prison Governor.
25 years' service.

MY one painting which says the most, at least to me, is this one. It's a sort of representation of a big rusty machine, all lopsided and cracked, to suggest it used to work but it was badly designed and began to break up, and all the metal split and the oil started to ooze out everywhere. To give the idea of what I was after, which is a symbolic self-portrait, it isn't oil coming out through the cracks though, it's blood.

> Dick M. (32)
> Offence: attempted murder.
> Sentence: 15 years.

What's all this 'communicate' crap?
I don't understand: voices
Hammer at me saying "Don't hate".
Well if I could understand that
Maybe I could communicate
And join your crew:
And be further misunderstood
And hated by you.

> Ron G. (26)
> Offence: possession of drugs.
> Sentence: 4 years.

Contemporary man sings tolerance,
And he sings that song to you and me.
But point out an error in his ways
And he says it's you who cannot see.

Contemporary man sings tolerance,
But there's something phoney in his song
For if your views don't match with his
He won't stay tolerant for long.

Contemporary man sings tolerance –
We're told that Jesus also sang it well:
Like "Heaven is yours if you believe in me –
But if you don't you'll go to Hell."

Ken L. (24)
Offence: assault on police.
Sentence: 4 years.

We are the dream-doers –
  Policemen hound and apprehend us,
  Judges to their prisons send us,
  Parole-boards think about and inspect us,
  Social workers try to correct us . . .

We are the dream-doers –
  Employment officials berate us,
  Retired colonels castigate us,
  Newspaper editors revile us,
  Bureaucrats want to rank and file us . . .

We are the dream-doers –
  We are the 'beatniks', the 'hippies', the 'beardies',
  We are the 'tuned-in', the 'turned-on', the 'weirdies',
  We are the drop-outs whom they scream of
Because we do the dreams they only dream of.

> Ron G. (26)
> Offence: possession of drugs.
> Sentence: 4 years.

I try to get through to people
Who've got two ears, using words
To try and make a connection.
But somehow it never seems to happen,
There's a web of complexity somewhere
Between that words get lost in
And I don't make myself clear
Or they don't understand.
We hardly get past the introduction
Before we start on the destruction.

Peter S. (28)
Offence: malicious wounding.
Sentence: 7 years.

THE incredible way time seems to stop moving all together, that was the thing I was least prepared for and haven't got used to even now. I'll be in the workshop and my mind'll be far away, thinking of the end of my sentence next year and all the things I'm going to do and the places I'm going to go, and then I suddenly come back with a jerk to where I am. I say to myself 'Oh well, all that helped to pass a bit of time'. Then I look up at the clock, and I see the hand's moved on exactly one minute since I looked at it before.

Stuart H. (24)
Offence: arson.
Sentence: 4 years.

IT'S waiting, that's all it is, waiting like sitting on a station-platform waiting for a train that's interminably bloody late. And all the time you're there you seem to be getting more and more hemmed-in with annoyance and aggravation and annoyance and aggravation on and on. You can't leave the platform for a break to go and look at the bookstall or have a cup of coffee, you've got to sit there and wait in fucking frustration and monotony.

> Bob D. (35)
> Offence: robbery with violence.
> Sentence: 10 years.

HOW could you describe monotony except by saying it's the same thing repeated over and over again until you're sick of it and going on being repeated over and over again until you're no longer even sick of it you're not anything only that doesn't stop it being repeated over and over again whether you're sick of it or you're not sick of it and whether you're anything or you're not anything and it still goes on being repeated over and over again . . . or something like that.

Paul M. (28)
Offence: grievous bodily harm.
Sentence: 6 years.

EXERCISE YARD

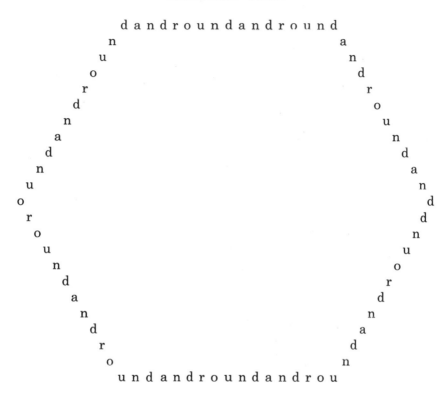

Malcolm J. (28)
Offence: fraud.
Sentence: 4 years.

OH you soon settle down. You don't have any responsibilities or worries, you don't have to take any decisions, it's like being reduced to a child again. They say childhood's the happiest time of your life. 'Happiness' would be inappropriate for the situation, but 'contented acceptance' would often be fairly near it.

> Trevor T. (49)
> Offence: fraud.
> Sentence: 8 years.

THE previous sentence I had to this one was eight years, and while I was doing it I spent all my time adjusting myself to life in prison because it was the only life I'd got. I'd just about perfected it when it was time for my release and I was thrown out. I didn't want to go, after all that effort at settling down. Luckily I was only out a few weeks before I was caught for something or other and put back in again. It only took me a few weeks to get back into the right state of mind and I've been O.K. now ever since.

Norman Y. (46)
Offence: housebreaking.
Sentence: 4 years.

I DON'T understand you, how do you mean, does time 'bother' me, how could it? I know it's something that's going on, something that's passing – but not in the same sense as it is to you. What you'd call a year means about as much as a fortnight or a month to me, that's all.

> Roger L. (31)
> Offence: armed robbery.
> Sentence: 12 years.

I CAN'T say the idea of having to stay here for the next twelve years or so concerns me very much. There might be a few people, but only a couple at the most, who'd be a bit perturbed about it if they thought of me but off-hand I couldn't even remember their names so from a personal point of view it doesn't matter really.

John R. (46)
Offence: murder.
Sentence: life.

I SEEM to remember time did play on my mind a bit when I first came in, which I suppose would be about ten years ago now, but it doesn't worry me anymore. What would today be, about Tuesday or Wednesday the sixteenth of something? Thursday the twenty-sixth? Well I'll take your word for it, and that'll illustrate the point I'm trying to make won't it?

>   Pat D. (42)
>   Offence: murder.
>   Sentence: life.

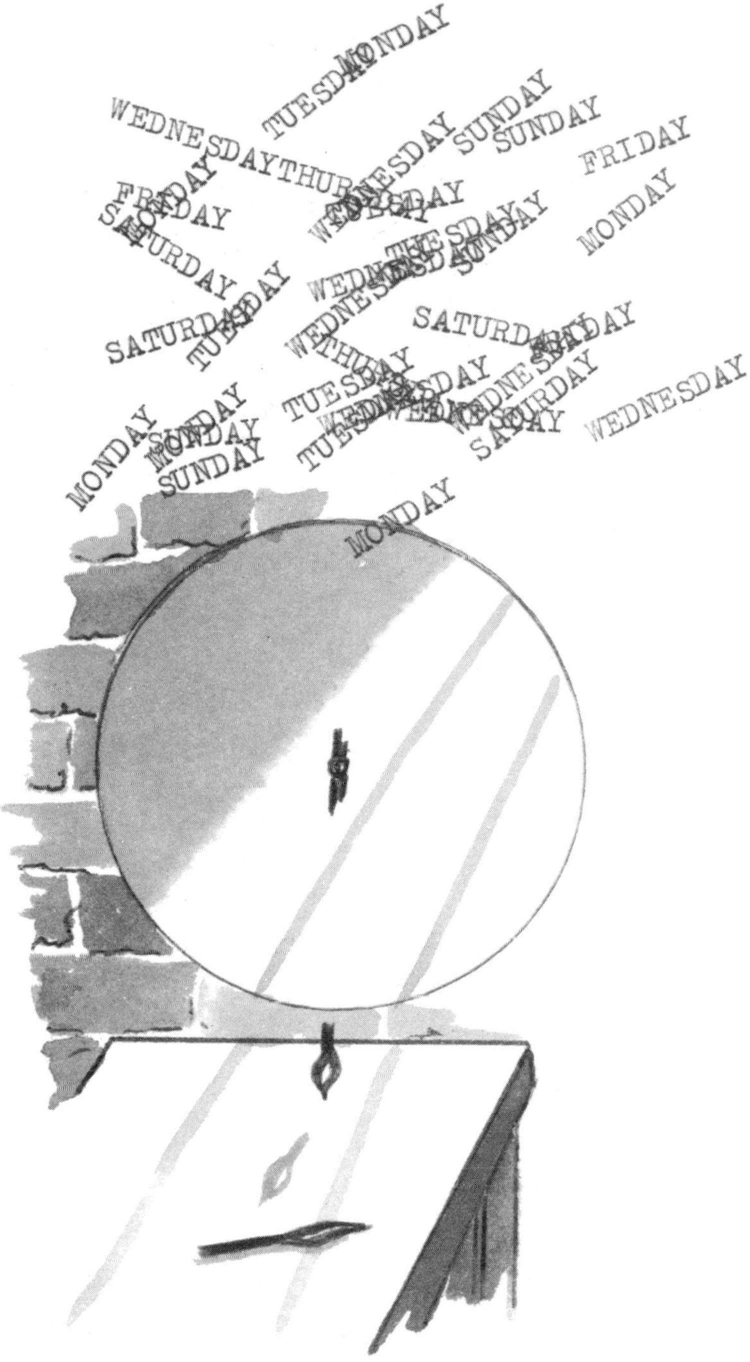
MONDAY
TUESDAY
WEDNESDAY
SUNDAY
SUNDAY
FRIDAY
MONDAY
FRIDAY
SATURDAY
SATURDAY
SATURDAY
WEDNESDAY
TUESDAY
MONDAY
SUNDAY
WEDNESDAY
MONDAY

It's been one of those kind of doomy years.

Guitar's stood there in that corner
Month's now, not had a touch. Books
On the shelf unopened, ignored, unread.
Nothing painted. Not drawn nothing much.
Spoke a few words but nothing of meaning said.
No thoughts no dreams no tears not a smile.
Just a sort of mood comes on you
Now and again, that's all, for a while.
Know how I mean? Somehow . . . lean.
Suppose it'll pass later or soon
Unnoticed, un-noted, unseen.

One of those kind of doomy years
This one's been.

> John E. (34)
> Offence: manslaughter.
> Sentence: 10 years.

NO, I've no idea how they decide when to let you out. One prisoner told me the thing to do was behave very badly for about five years and then start to behave better, so they'd think you were making progress. Another one said it was best to be a model prisoner right from the start. Then you meet someone who's done just that and you find he's been in fifteen years so far and still's got no idea when he's going out, and another chap who's been a bloody nuisance and that everybody hates and suddenly you find he's given a release-date. You hear rumours and tales all the time, not just from prisoners but the staff too. There was a screw said to me once no one was ever let out under thirty-five, and another one equally definite said the ones who had the best chance were those who were around thirty. So don't ask me: for all I know the system might be simply drawing numbers out of a hat.

Roy S. (48)
Offence: murder.
Sentence: life.

A LIFE sentence has no fixed length you see, it's an indefinite period so there's no point in making plans of any sort for going out. I don't even know if I'm going to be let out, never mind when. So for instance a word like 'tomorrow' doesn't have any meaning to me except in the way that tomorrow might be my day for having a bath or changing library books. But no more than that. I told somebody that once and he said it was being unrealistic. I don't, I think it's being realistic.

Ray T. (35)
Offence: murder.
Sentence: life.

THE only sort of way I could
tell you about myself, how I
am, doing this length of time, I
suppose it would be to get a cup of
water and float a burnt-out match
on it and say sit and watch it, see
how it got water-logged and
gradually got lower and lower
sinking under the surface, that'd be
about it, how it is, that'd be me.

Len B. (45)
Offence: manslaughter.
Sentence: 15 years.

Due to a general lack of interest
Tomorrow has been cancelled
And in its place will be
A continuous repetition of today.
Which may be very monotonous
But definitely seems to be
In response to public demand.

> Trevor T. (49)
> Offence: fraud.
> Sentence: 8 years.

IT follows you around as though you'd got a dog tied to you on the end of a piece of string. You forget it for a while that you've got this long sentence, then it suddenly bites you in the ankle when you're not expecting it. When I do go out eventually I'll never have a dog and take it walks, it'd be too much of a symbolic sort of reminder.

Len B. (45)
Offence: manslaughter.
Sentence: 15 years.

IT'S something I don't seem able to get the knack of, either I'm unlucky or not very clever, I'm not sure which. Other men have succeeded first time but I've had three or four goes and not managed it. The tie broke that I'd fixed-up like a noose from the cell-window bars, then another time a knife I'd nicked from the canteen and spent nights sharpening-up with a bit of stone so I could have a go at this vein in my wrist, all it did was a lot of blood came out but the vein was too deep or something it wouldn't cut it properly. I suppose there must be a way of doing it certain, and I try to copy the ones I've heard of where it's worked but you can't ask them afterwards how they got it right because they're not here. Anyway thinking about it and trying to solve how to do it properly, it does give me something to occupy my mind with otherwise I'd have nothing to think about, I'd go mad.

Colin M. (38)
Offence: arson, manslaughter.
Sentence: 20 years.

A WORLD of its own and a world of dreams, and all the men locked-up in it keep some part of themselves locked-up inside themselves too where no-one else can get at it.

John E. (34)
Offence: manslaughter.
Sentence: 10 years.

I won't get sick
Of being in nick
Even if things are what they seem.
It's such a good place to dream
Of what was or will be or might have been . . .

The sound of cultured voices.
Maroon Rolls Royces.
Hand-rolled cigars.
Five-star bars.
Pretty girls
In mink and pearls.
A big house in Weybridge, Surrey –
Oh yes of course and naturally
No financial worry.

Peter D. (28)
Offence: larceny.
Sentence: 3 years.

I LIKE the night. It's the only private time, the time when I'm completely alone and can think, or not think and let my mind wander, and no one can stop me or interfere. Me and the night are friends, real good friends, in fact I'd say the night was the best friend I've ever had.

> Roger L. (31)
> Offence: armed robbery.
> Sentence: 12 years.

Still
    after all these years
      I shape myself for sleep
        as though you were beside me
          my arm curved to pillow your head
            my knee bent to fit between your thighs –
        still
      after
    all
  these
years.

Andy K. (36)
Offence: armed robbery.
Sentence: 8 years.

IT'S never done me no good and I
don't see how it could do
anybody any good. The truth of it
is that you go in bad and you come
out ten times bloody worse.

Steve P. (35)
Offence: possessing firearms.
Sentence: 5 years.

DOING my time I just let the routine take over and give myself up completely to dreams and practical thoughts. Dreams of the really big job I'm going to pull next time, and practical thoughts about how to do it in a way I won't get caught. I mean otherwise it wouldn't be worth being in prison, you might as well give up crime all together if you're not going to put your time to good use inside while you've got the opportunity to think things out carefully and see where you went wrong last time and make sure you'll not make the same mistakes again.

Ralph H. (33)
Offence: housebreaking.
Sentence: 4 years.

I'VE found it a lot of help for learning. When I was first put away it was to approved school for nicking a load of flower pots which was difficult to get rid of and you don't get a lot for them. Then I went to borstal for something else stupid, but at least while I was in borstal I learned how to open doors properly. Then when I got to prison I was taught how to open bigger things, like warehouses and safes and things. I'd say that by now over the years I've more or less learned everything I could want to know, like how to climb stack-pipes, pick locks, blow safes without making a noise about it, put alarm-systems out of action and so on, and all of it practical useful stuff that's always coming in very handy. This is because I've studied and I'm a good learner and I've had the teaching from men who are real masters of their trade.

Jack K. (36)
Offence: housebreaking.
Sentence: 4 years.

ALL these places do for me is make me determined to hit back harder than ever when I get out. I've a chip on my shoulder, yes, but I don't think I had it so much when I first started being sent to prison, in those days I used to feel I probably deserved it. That's all gone long-since now though, all I've got is this big hatred for what's called straight society, and it's been going into prison such a lot that has turned me like that.

> Les M. (34)
> Offence: housebreaking.
> Sentence: 6 years.

SOCIETY'S an organisation, right? And if you want a man to join it but you make him afraid of it and see it'll go on being vindictive towards him until he does join it, well I can't see how he's going to be much good to you even if you do get him to join it eventually. He'll have joined through fear, not because he wants to. All you'll have got is a no-good man, a weak man who can be scared into things. I wouldn't think any organisation wants people like that because they could just as easily be scared out of membership again.

Ron G. (26)
Offence: possession of drugs.
Sentence: 4 years.

GOD knows I've been punished often enough ever since I can remember, but this punishment you've been dishing out to me and thousands of others, can't you see it's completely lost its usefulness by now even if it had any in the first place? It doesn't deter me, it doesn't frighten me, all it does is grind me down and destroy me as a person and leave me as a nothing. It could've been that once there was something in me, perhaps only a little, but something that was worthwhile; only if there was, it's been wiped-out completely. If that was what you intended and what you wanted, to get rid of any spark of anything good in me at all, why take so long over it and spend so much time and money and trouble on it? Why didn't you just take me out and shoot me in the first place?

> Mike O. (40)
> Offence: warehouse breaking.
> Sentence: 4 years.

If you expect remorse you'll be disappointed:
All you'll get is regret-at-being-caught.
If you expect redemption you'll be disappointed:
All you'll get is determination-to-do-it-right-next-time.
If you expect pleas for forgiveness you'll be disappointed:
All you'll get is desire-to-exact-retribution.
Don't expect too much and then you won't be
    disappointed:
Just hatred. Expect that, just that, and then for sure
You'll be in no danger of being disappointed.

Andy K. (36)
Offence: armed robbery.
Sentence: 8 years.

I ACCEPT I can't exist outside without getting into trouble, and you have to accept it too. Well obviously you do accept it, because that's why you keep putting me back inside. Whichever way it's looked at, by me or you, I should have thought that means I'm not normal. Not abnormal enough to be put in the nut-house, but definitely out-of-gear, not up to it, not properly equipped – maybe like somebody's who's blind or has only got one leg. Well with a blind person you try and guide him, with someone who's only got one leg you fix him up with an artificial one so he can at least stand up and try to learn to walk. But with someone like me who's always getting into trouble, stealing and doing things like that, all you do's lock him up and forget about him for a bit – until he comes out and steals again, and then you lock him up some more. It doesn't seem you're making any progress, I'm making any progress, or anyone's making any progress. We're all getting nowhere, fast. You're just as much blind and one-legged persons as I am.

Ted R. (35)
Offence: warehouse breaking.
Sentence: 3 years.

I'M what's called a recidivist, a repeating offender, a habitual wrong-doer. I know something's wrong with me but I'm buggered if I know what it is anymore than you do. But I spend more time trying to puzzle it out than you because it affects me much more, I'm the one who's doing the time locked-up in these places. I don't seem able to do anything to change myself when I get out, and whether you believe me or not, I honestly do wish I could. But I can't, not on my own, I need help: a hell of a lot of help, and patience, and no expectation that I'll change completely overnight, because I know I won't, it won't be as easy as that either for me or for you. I'm stuck in a way of thinking that I can't climb out of on my own.

Harry M. (42)
Offence: fraud.
Sentence: 12 years.

IF a man gets knocked unconscious, say a boxer or someone who's been in a road accident or something, even if it's only been just for one minute, they treat him very careful afterwards because they know it's not a good thing to happen to someone. For all we know it might not be a good thing to happen to someone that he should be in prison, perhaps not even for one day, it might have effects on him we don't know anything about. Only nobody studies this, not even thinks of studying this, which seems a funny way of going on to me because after all putting people in prison is deliberate, it's not an accident. But they very carefully studies the result of an accident only not the result of something deliberate if you know what I mean.

Bernard L. (52)
Offence: housebreaking.
Sentence: 8 years.

It's humans that they put in prison.
It's humans that puts humans in prison.
It's humans that puts humans in prison because
They say they're not humans they're animals.
But I don't know any animals that puts animals in prison.

Eddie S. (47)
Offence: indecent assault.
Sentence: 8 years.

SOMEBODY like me who's an "A List" man is somebody who it's been decided would be very very dangerous for the public if he ever escaped. I have precautions that are extra-strict taken for me, I can't move about so much inside the prison like the others, there's a special careful watch kept on me day and night. No I don't know why it's called the "A List", I don't know what the "A" stands for, unless perhaps it's 'animal'.

Alf B. (50)
Offence: rape.
Sentence: life.

ONE thing that really does puzzle me is why society seems to think prison's a universal cure-all for so many different types of behaviour – sex-crimes, murder, embezzlement, petty thieving, pushing drugs, bouncing dud-cheques, spur-of-the-moment idiocies or carefully-thought-out robberies. It's not like in medicine where you've got different treatments for different illnesses and very much depending on what they are. Millions of pounds are spent on finding the right way of dealing with each individual thing, there's no one panacea that'll deal with everything whatever its cause or its symptoms might be.

Actually though I don't think society does see it like that; it doesn't want prison to be anything but retributive. But the fact it doesn't have any good effect and only makes people worse doesn't seem to worry it at all.

Walter C. (54)
Offence: embezzlement.
Sentence: 6 years.

YOU'LL have heard it said almost as many times as I have, God knows it's said often enough, I suppose on the principle that if you go on repeating a thing long enough everyone'll believe it, that after-care begins on the day a man first comes into prison. It might be true for all I know; but it's equally true that it stops on the day he goes out. The only sort of long-term after-care I've ever known about is being put back in prison.

Victor G. (40)
Offence: armed robbery.
Sentence: 10 years.

IT'S bad coming in, but you can get used to it. What's much worse and what I can't ever get used to though is going out. That really is bloody terrible. When they opened the door in the gate for me last time I had to cling to it for a minute to sort of steady myself, I felt like I was stepping off the edge of a cliff into the sea. I was so frightened I wanted to turn round and run straight back to my cell and hide, because that was somewhere where I knew I'd be safe and there was nothing to be scared of.

Ron C. (39)
Offence: housebreaking.
Sentence: 5 years.

THIS is my first day out. I feel rotten, I suppose it's because I had such a terrible night last night. Nice comfortable bed in a nice comfortable furnished room, the very thing I'd been looking forward to so long. But I couldn't get used to it at all, just lay there staring at the ceiling, closing my eyes every few minutes hoping I'd go to sleep, opening a book, smoking cigarettes, getting up and walking round, lying down again. Bloody hopeless it was. Went on like that a good three or four hours before it dawned on me what was the matter. Know what it was? I was lying there waiting for someone to switch the light off, never crossed my mind I could do it myself.

Bert W. (55)
After 6-year sentence.

PRISON'S complete conditioning, I suppose you get out of it in time but I don't know how long it takes. For instance you're woken up every morning at half-past six. Well I've been out four years but I still wake up every morning at half-past six. Your cell light's put out at nine o'clock – and at nine o'clock every night I go to bed, I can't stay up because my eyes seem to close automatically.

Mick M. (46)
After 6-year sentence.

I'LL have been out seven years next month. I can still hear that cell door being slammed to and shutting me in for the night, the absolutely final sound of it like a big metal shutter coming down between me and the world. I've always got the edgy feeling that at any moment it's going to happen, perhaps even in the middle of our conversation. Suddenly there'll be this terrific clang, something'll drop between us, I won't be able to see you or hear you, I'll be shut up in complete isolation with no way out.

George H. (45)
After 10-year sentence.

IT'S just over eight years. I'm married to a lovely wife, we've two lovely kids, a nice home, I've a decent job. But there are still a lot of things I can't do and I don't suppose I'll ever be able to. Like staying in a room if there's a clock with a loud tick in it, or eating off a metal plate of any kind. I can't sleep in a bed if my wife's not in it, I can't stand being in places where there's lots of people milling about. Things I can't bring myself to face, like if the kids want to go to the zoo like they do sometimes. I won't go, my wife has to take them on her own, I don't want to stand looking at animals in cages.

Bill A. (50)
After 8-year sentence.

154

THERE'S a part of him that's somehow lost, that I can't ever get near to. It's nine years since now but sometimes he gets a kind of a look on his face and he sits and he doesn't speak or anything, he doesn't even seem to hear things being said to him. I used to ask him what he was thinking about but he'd never say, so now I don't. I know, and I just wait, it's as though I'm standing outside the gates waiting for him. It scares me sometimes because it lasts so long, I start to feel I might be losing him back in there for good.

> Wife of ex-prisoner
> released from life sentence.

I DON'T have any control over it, it'll happen
sometimes in the middle of an evening, perhaps when
I've gone out somewhere to people who've got no idea
about me. Suddenly I'm not there anymore, or they're
not there, everything's unreal. I suppose they must
think I'm a bit mental, I've 'gone off' or something. But
it doesn't feel like that to me, it's as though I'd been
'taken off' more like, by something I'm powerless to do
anything about. It's not that I'm lost in thought; I'm
just lost.

Neville D. (56)
Released from life sentence.

I can only say that even though I've been out for twelve years, if it suddenly happened for some reason that I had to go back to prison tomorrow again for a long time, I'd feel nothing, I'd simply accept it. That's what being in prison did for me.

John W. (54)
After 15-year sentence.

Listen.
To the wind say nothing.
Listen to the wind say nothing.
Hear nothing.
Let the wind hear nothing.
Everything is very still.
Is the world empty?
I think it must be.
In this prison-place
The silence is full of shrieking
That nobody hears,
That the wind does not carry
For anyone to hear.
Perhaps hearing nothing
On the wind
They think there is nothing
To hear.
Perhaps it is that those
Outside cannot hear it
That is the real hellishness
Of hell.

Geoff B. (21)
Offence: murder.
Sentence: life.